Black Bears

NORTHWORD
Minnetonka, Minnesota

DEDICATION
To Panky Snow, a great friend and a wonderful writer

© NorthWord Press, 2000

Photography © 2000: Michael H. Francis: front cover, pp. 5, 12, 34, 42-43, 44; Donald M. Jones: pp. 4, 6-7, 10-11, 28; Bill Lea: pp. 8, 15, 17, 18-19, 26-27, 37, 39; Rita Groszmann: pp. 16, 23, 30-31, 35, 40-41; Howie Garber/ www.wanderlustimages.com: pp. 20-21; Robert McCaw: p. 25; Lisa & Mike Husar/Team Husar: pp. 32-33; Mark Raycroft: p. 36; John R. Ford: back cover.

Illustrations by John F. McGee
Designed by Russell S. Kuepper
Edited by Barbara K. Harold

NorthWord
11571 K-Tel Drive
Minnetonka, MN 55343
www.tnkidsbooks.com

Library of Congress Cataloging-in-Publication Data

Feeney, Kathy.
    Black bears / by Kathy Feeney ; illustrations by John F. McGee.
        p. cm. -- (Our wild world series)
    ISBN 1-55971-742-4 (soft cover)
    ISBN 13: 978-1-55971-742-7
    1. Black bear--Juvenile literature. [1. Black bear. 2. Bears.] I. McGee, John F. II. Title.
III. Series.

QL737.C27 F45 2000
599.78--dc21
                                                                00-028384

Printed in Malaysia

Our WILD™ WORLD SERIES

Black Bears

Kathy Feeney
Illustrations by John F. McGee

NORTHWORD
Minnetonka, Minnesota

SOME PEOPLE fear the mighty black bear. They know bears are extremely strong, with sharp claws and dangerous teeth. But most black bears are actually shy and solitary mammals. They avoid contact with people and even other bears. They prefer to be left alone!

There are eight species (SPEE-sees), or kinds, of bear. They are the North American black bear, the Asiatic black bear, the brown (or grizzly) bear, the giant panda, the polar bear, the sloth bear, the spectacled bear, and the sun bear.

They all may belong to the same family, but there are many differences between these bear types. They live in different parts of the world. For example, the spectacled bear is found in South America and the Asiatic black bear lives in Asia. They are also different in size. The brown bear is very large and the sun bear is quite small. Most bears move quickly but the sloth bear moves very slowly.

Even the large black bear moves quietly in its forest home.

Young bears are only playing when they nip at each other.

Another difference may be their coat colors. But no matter what color a bear's coat is, it works like camouflage (KAM-uh-flaj). It protects the bear by helping it blend into its natural habitat. This helps it hide from predators, or enemies.

Polar bears, for example, have yellowish-white fur. They are hard to see in their snowy Arctic surroundings. Giant pandas are both black and white. This color combination helps them blend into the shadowy mountain forests of China.

Black bears are almost always black with tan muzzles, or snouts. They also can be dark brown, cinnamon, or tan. Sometimes they have a white patch of hair on their throat or chest.

North American black bears are the most common bear species in the world today. They live only in North America. Many of their woodland and mountain habitats are also inhabited by humans. This is the kind of bear that people are most likely to see in the wild.

Bears often travel through wide open spaces,
and can quickly "disappear" into nearby trees.

This mother and baby are different colors,
but they are both North American black bears.

The area where a bear lives is called its home range, or territory. The size of the territory depends on the amount of food it has for the bear. If there is little food, a bear needs a larger territory to find enough to eat. It could be as small as 3 square miles (7.8 square kilometers) or as large as 10 square miles (26 square kilometers). A bear usually protects and stays in the same territory its whole life. But bears do not choose one place to live inside this area. They prefer to roam, or wander, throughout their home range. They may sleep in a different place each night.

A young female black bear often chooses her territory near her mother's home range. Young males usually travel far from their mother's territory to find their own home range.

Bears are diurnal (die-YER-nul), meaning they move around during the day and at night. When bears become tired, they stop right where they are to rest. They often make a bed of grass and leaves in the shade. A thicket of bushes makes a safe place for sleeping. A pile of rocks or a cave also provides good hidden shelter. Females with babies, called cubs, often rest near a tree so the young can quickly climb the tree to escape danger.

Black Bears
FUNFACT:

The scientific name for the
North American black bear is
Ursus americanus.

Pages 10-11: A spruce tree provides a safe place for this bear cub to wait for its mother.

Black bears can grow to about 6 feet (1.8 meters) long. They weigh as much as 200 to 600 pounds (91 to 272 kilograms). Some bears have weighed more than 800 pounds (360 kilograms). Males are called boars. They are larger and heavier than females, which are called sows.

A bear's long, thick body is very muscular and athletic under its heavy coat of hair. Its tail is short and stubby. Its head is large. Black bears have small eyes with poorer eyesight than many other animals. But they can distinguish colors and see movement. Bears have small, round ears and their hearing is very good. They can hear many high-pitched sounds that humans cannot hear.

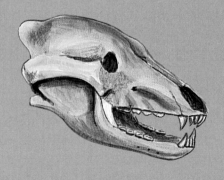

When they stand upright, bears look even bigger and more dangerous.

A bear's sense of smell, with its long snout and black nose, is excellent. Bears usually walk slowly and stop often, lifting their snouts into the air to sniff for food or danger. Scientists estimate that a bear's sense of smell is 15 times greater than a person's sense of smell. Bears can sniff food from more than 3 miles (4.8 kilometers) away. That would be like a person being able to smell cookies baking in a house across town!

Even though black bears have short legs, they can run in bursts up to 30 miles (48 kilometers) per hour. That's as fast as a horse, and much faster than a human.

Bears are also strong swimmers. They do the "dog-paddle" to cross a river, lake, or stream. Bears may use the water to cool off in the warm weather, and as a way to escape predators. When a bear leaves the water, it usually shakes its soaked coat, just like a big wet dog. This removes water and dirt from its fur.

A bear also may lick its coat clean. Sometimes bears roll around in the mud. They do this to get rid of fleas! When bears feel itchy from a fly or an insect bite, they scratch their fur against the bark of a tree. You might be able to tell if a bear has been in the area by looking for clumps of bear hair stuck to the trunk of a tree.

Sometimes people say they are "as hungry as a bear." That's because bears eat so much and so often. In fact, they spend most of their day searching for things to eat.

More than 80 percent of a bear's diet is plants. They often eat berries, fruit, flowers, and many kinds of nuts, including acorns. They also consume grasses, twigs, and roots. But bears are omnivores (OM-ni-vorz), which means they eat both plants and meat. Bears eat many insects and sometimes they eat animals such as mice or squirrels.

Black Bears
FUNFACT:

An adult bear can reach an
apple on a tree branch
7 to 8 feet above the ground.

This black bear's sense of smell probably led it
to search for food in this hollow tree stump.

Soapberries make a tasty snack for a hungry bear.

Bears may wade into streams and rivers to catch fish with their feet, or paws. They stick their long, sensitive tongues into tree trunks to catch ants and termites. Bears also eat tree sap. To get sap, they scratch the bark off a tree. Then they lick the tree as the sweet sap oozes from inside. It is the same sap that people collect to make syrup for their pancakes.

People can guess what a bear ate by the color of its droppings, or scat. It may be purplish, for example, after the bear has eaten blueberries.

Scat is usually dark in color and looks like a pile of marbles with some berries in it. If the bear has consumed ripe apples, the scat is lighter and looks mushy. The scat of a bear that has been eating fish has fish scales in it.

You can tell the bear ate cranberries by looking at these droppings.

Bears know that ants and other insects can be found under rocks.

Honey is a favorite food. Bears get their honey fresh from bee nests. These nests are called beehives. When bears find beehives hanging in trees, they climb the tree and scoop the thick, golden honey out of the hive with their big paws. Then they eat the honey and the entire nest, including the bees. The bees often sting the bears but that doesn't keep them from looking for another beehive!

Bears also dig up roots and use their claws to find insects in hollow logs. They even turn over large rocks to find food underneath them.

Black Bears
FUNFACT:

In their strong jaw, bears have 42 teeth, which easily crush, grind, and tear food. Humans have 32 teeth.

Bears are excellent at fishing, and this salmon will make a good meal.

Scientists who study animals are called zoologists (zoe-OL-uh-jists). They have learned that bears have excellent memories. Just as people remember the names of their favorite restaurants, bears remember places where they have found tasty meals. Somehow they remember how to get there and when the food is ready to eat. They often return to the same location year after year. When young bears are shown the routes or trails to these good feeding areas, they begin using them too.

Eating huge amounts of food in the summer and fall is one way black bears prepare for winter. In fact, they overeat on purpose to gain extra weight—often more than 100 pounds (45 kilograms). Bears need a thick layer of fat for warmth and nourishment during the winter.

Another way to prepare for winter is for the bear to grow a thick layer of fur under its softer, lighter summer coat. In the spring, the bear sheds this fur to keep cooler in the warm weather of summer. The top layer is made up of long, shiny hairs called guard hairs.

Black Bears
FUNFACT:

People eat about 1,500 calories each day. In the fall, a bear may consume 15,000 calories each day!

Just before winter, bears look very fat and ready for a long sleep.

By the end of fall, each bear must find a place to sleep through the winter. Bears often use a cave or fallen hollow tree. Bears also dig a hole in the ground. These homes, called dens, provide both shelter and safety until spring.

The size of the den depends on the size of the bear. A bear needs just enough room to turn around inside the den. A larger den would waste precious body heat. Bears usually sleep in a den only one winter. They find a new one each year.

This winter sleep is called hibernation (hi-ber-NAY-shun). Bears hibernate to conserve energy. They do this because vegetation and other food sources are extremely scarce during cold weather, especially if there is snow on the ground.

Most bears do not even eat or drink during their hibernation. Some bears in the warmer areas of North America occasionally leave the den for a short time. Then they go back to hibernating.

During hibernation, a bear's metabolism (meh-TAB-o-liz-um) decreases. This means its heartbeat, blood flow, and breathing are slower. Somehow bears remain healthy and their muscles stay strong until they emerge (ee-MERJ), or come out of the den, in the spring.

There are many mysteries about black bear hibernation that zoologists continue to study.

Deep snow often camouflages the entrance to a bear den.

Bear cubs learn to stay together when their mother is away.

Bears do not usually live together in groups. Even after adults breed in the summer, they go their separate ways. Boars do not stay around to help the sows raise their cubs.

That means when a sow is going to have babies she must find a safe site, or location, for a den by herself. She carefully makes a soft bed with nearby leaves and twigs. She knows that her cubs will be born in about January. This happens while the sow is still hibernating!

Black Bears
FUNFACT:

Bear species are found everywhere in the world except Australia, Africa, and Antarctica.

Most adult bears have few enemies to worry about in their home territory.

Black bears give birth only once every two years. Sows may have as many as four cubs at a time. The group is called a litter. A newborn bear cub is smaller than a squirrel. Each one weighs about 10 ounces (283 grams) and measures about 8 inches (20 centimeters) long.

Bears are born bald and toothless. But they already have claws.

After the mother gives birth, she licks her cubs clean. Bear cubs get nourishment from drinking their mother's milk. They stay warm snuggling against their mother's fur. The mother and her newborns remain together in the den until spring.

By then each cub weighs nearly 8 pounds (4 kilograms). They have tasted only their mother's milk. They are fat, furry, and eager to leave their den.

When adult bears finally emerge in the spring, they are very hungry and thirsty. They have lost weight during hibernation and are ready to eat again!

Cubs learn many important things from their mother, like how to find food.

The mother bear spends this first summer teaching her cubs many things. She shows them how to eat new foods and where to find them.

Cubs learn to carefully watch their mother at all times. If there is danger, she warns them to quickly climb a nearby tree. And she signals to them when it is safe to come down. She often climbs the tree with them to avoid danger on the ground.

Bear cubs are very curious. They are playful and want to discover their new world. If they wander too far away from their mother, she calls them back with grunts.

She may also "woof" like a dog to warn them of predators such as eagles, bobcats, and wolves. Sometimes even adult male bears are dangerous to young bears.

Splashing through a stream keeps these bear cubs
cool in the warm summer sunshine.

When the weather turns cold, the mother bear and her cubs find a new den and spend a second winter together. This time, the cubs hibernate too.

In the spring when these cubs emerge from the den, they are called yearlings. They usually leave their mother for good the following summer.

Bear siblings, or brothers and sisters, sometimes continue to live together after they leave their mother. By a year later, they each go their own way and are completely on their own.

Black Bears
FUNFACT:

The bear is related to the dog, the fox, and the wolf.

Climbing a tree, even a small one, keeps this cub safe from predators.

We may not understand bear "talk," but cubs do!

Some claw marks are deep and easy to see, since a black bear's claws may be 2 inches (5 centimeters) long.

Bears keep in touch by snorting, whining, and making a sound like a roar. Bears can communicate silently in several ways too. When its ears are straight up, a bear is at ease. If they are laid back, the bear is probably angry, especially at a misbehaving cub.

Bears also claw tree trunks. These scratches tell other bears to keep out of their territory.

Sniffing the air is a way for a black bear to know if other bears are in the area. Each bear has its own unique scent (SENT), or odor.

During the breeding season, adult male bears rub their scent on trees to attract a mate. That scent is also in a bear's scat and in its tracks.

This bear may be sniffing the air for trespassers as it marks its territory.

One way for people to know if a bear has been in the area is to see its tracks on the ground. Each black bear paw has five toes and five sharp, curved claws. The back, or hind, tracks usually measure about 4 inches (10 centimeters) wide and 8 inches (20 centimeters) long. The front tracks are smaller.

The end of the track with the claw mark points in the direction that the bear was traveling. If the tracks are close together the bear was probably walking slowly. The farther apart the tracks are, the faster the bear was walking or running.

The black bear's flat and wide paws help it stand upright on its hind legs. Sometimes bears stand straight up to grab food out of trees or to get a better view. The fur and padding on the bottom of the paws help the bear travel quietly.

Black Bears
FUNFACT:

Two star constellations are named for bears: Ursa Major ("Great Bear") and Ursa Minor ("Little Bear"). They also are known as The Big Dipper and The Little Dipper.

Bears often leave a trail with their paw prints,
and you can tell which way they went.

A mother bear may attack if an enemy bothers her cubs. She guards them well.

Black bears can be dangerous if they are disturbed while eating.

Bears are peaceful by nature. But they may attack if they are surprised. A mother bear will fight off any predators that threaten her cubs.

An angry bear lowers its head and stares at its enemy with its ears flat back. The bear then slaps the ground with its paws and clicks its teeth before charging. Sometimes bears fight standing on their hind legs. When most animals see a bear's enormous body, huge teeth, and sharp claws, they quickly leave!

Black Bears
FUNFACT:

Early pioneers used black bear hair for fishing lures, and to stuff mattresses and pillows. Bear fat was even recommended as a cure for baldness!

Living in good habitat, this cub may live up to twenty-five years.

Zoologists estimate that there are about 500,000 black bears in North America. And the bear populations in some areas of the United States are growing steadily.

But the loss of good habitat is a threat to bear survival in other areas. When people build houses in the forests where bears live, the bears lose their natural homes and many die.

Our national parks and forests have habitats that will never be destroyed. And bears living there will always have good territories to roam.

Fortunately, there are many people who respect the North American black bear and work very hard to protect its habitat and food sources. This will help the bear survive and continue to live in the wild.

Black Bears
FUNFACT:

Native Americans believed bears were sacred animals. They wore bear-tooth necklaces for good luck.

Internet Sites

You can find out more interesting information about black bears and lots of other wildlife by visiting these Internet sites.

www.animal.discovery.com — Discovery Channel Online

www.bear.org — North American Bear Center

www.bearbiology.com — International Association for Bear Research and Management

www.kidsplanet.org — Defenders of Wildlife

www.nationalgeographic.com/kids — National Geographic Society

www.nwf.org/kids — National Wildlife Federation

www.worldwildlife.org — World Wildlife Fund

http://nature.org/ — The Nature Conservancy

Index

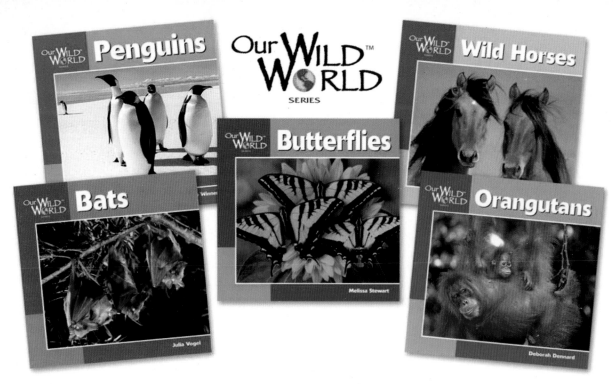

Titles available in the Our Wild World Series:

NorthWord
Minnetonka, Minnesota